THE DAMNED

VOLUME 1, "THREE DAYS DEAD"

THE DAM

NED™

VOLUME 1, "THREE DAYS DEAD"

Written by
CULLEN BUNN

Illustrated by
BRIAN HURTT

Colored by
BILL CRABTREE

Lettered by
CRANK!

Designed by
KEITH WOOD

Edited by
CHARLIE CHU

ONI PRESS

AN ONI PRESS PUBLICATION

THE DAMNED: THREE DAYS DEAD
Original series edited by Randal C. Jarrell

Published by Oni Press, Inc.
Joe Nozemack, publisher
James Lucas Jones, editor in chief
Andrew McIntire, v.p. of marketing & sales
David Dissanayake, sales manager
Rachel Reed, publicity coordinator
Troy Look, director of design & production
Hilary Thompson, graphic designer
Angie Dobson, digital prepress technician
Ari Yarwood, managing editor
Charlie Chu, senior editor
Robin Herrera, editor
Bess Pallares, editorial assistant
Brad Rooks, director of logistics
Jung Lee, logistics associate

Oni Press, Inc
1305 SE Martin Luther King, Jr. Blvd
Suite A
Portland, OR 97214

onipress.com
facebook.com/onipress · twitter.com/onipress
onipress.tumblr.com · instagram.com/onipress

cullenbunn.com · @cullenbunn
brihurtt.com · @brihurtt · instagram.com/brihurtt · tabletitans.com
@crabtree_bill
@ccrank

First edition: March 2017
ISBN 978-1-62010-385-2
eISBN 978-1-62010-386-9

Library of Congress Control Number: 2016951885

10 9 8 7 6 5 4 3 2 1

Printed in China

Lemme guess.

You're one of those guys thinks he's got it all figured. You run your little grifts, call in a few ill-earned favors, and never make a promise unless there's something bigger and better in it for you.

Well, I'm gonna help you out and let you in on a little secret — not the real secret, mind you... this is just the tip of the tombstone. You see, you think you've got an edge over everybody else in the smarts department... and the families love guys like you. You're pretty sure you know every trick in the book and can weasel your way out of any problem. But what you don't know is you're dealing with the oldest tricksters to ever put on a pinstripe, and they always collect on their bargains.

I should know. I was just like you.

Maybe you're thinking if I tried to pull a few fast ones and lived to tell about it, you might get lucky, too.

Make no mistake, there's nothing lucky about my situation.

I got one thing and one thing only pulling for me.

Sometimes, the only person you can trust is a dead man.

CHAPTER
1

They say
dead men tell
no tales...

...but that just
ain't so for
some of us.

Excuse me waiter, but there's a fly in my—

Shaddup.

You shoulda known better than to play the double-cross, Dutch.

Ptu!

Took you guys long enough.

I smell like *shit*.

How long have I been out here?

Not nearly long enough, Eddie.

No, thanks. I've been off my feet for a bit, so I don't mind walking.

Don't make this *rougher* than it needs to be.

What's wrong? Leave something *behind?*

Shake a leg. We need to get you *prettied up* for yer appointment.

Appointment?

"Yeah. The *boss* wants to see you."

Alphonse Aligheri.

He's everything you might expect in a crime boss. Cunning... ruthless...

Pretty much a complete sonovabitch.

Big Al?

Eddie! Come in and take a load off!

How ya been?

Dead.

But you knew that already, so why waste your breath asking?

15

...not to mention, he's a *demon*.

No law against being courteous to an old friend, is there?

We're friends again, is that it? Last I heard, you didn't care if I lived or died.

Makes a guy wonder *why* you pulled him out of the gutter.

You're an ungrateful piece of work, you know that, Eddie?

As far as I'm concerned, the world's a better place without you in it.

The boss here wants to dust you off, though, so that's fine by me.

But you're *bent* if you think I'm gonna let you spit in his face.

Now, Tony, I'm sure Eddie didn't mean to ruffle our feathers.

I meant what I said.

You must need me for something or you'd have left me to *rot*.

And muzzle your mutt already.

I've only been here a minute, and I've already had an earful of his yapping.

Why you—

Tony, maybe you should take some air.

Y'know, blow off a little steam.

Yeah. Run yourself a nice bath maybe.

17

Tony's getting touchy in his old age. Maybe you're working him too hard.

SLAM!

You've made a lot of enemies around town, Eddie, and you don't want to count Tony—or me—among them.

So we're talking about letting bygones be bygones?

We're talking about **opportunities.**

It's no secret, you and me, we've had our differences. But your...*talents* make you valuable to my organization.

You mean you don't have to worry about me getting whacked...

...and if I do, you can just dust me off and put me back on the job.

Ask me, the *Verlochin* did you a favor, cursing you the way they did.

Remind me to send them a thank you card...

Here's the thing, Eddie.

Me and *Bruno Roarke*, we've been working on a *deal* that'll put an end to our squabbles over territories once and for all.

Meaning you finally muscled old Bruno into rolling over.

Call it a *mutually beneficial* agreement.

Sounds real peaceful. Where do I fit in?

There's a lot of *red tape* comes with negotiations of this nature. *Outside parties* are required to finalize the deal.

But the demon sent to make the arrangements *vanished* right out from under our noses.

This missing demon got a name?

Lazlo.

He's a big shot, I gather.

High Order.

19

And you don't think he just got the urge to go *sight-seeing*, do you?

You think he got *pinched*.

That's what I want *you* to find out, real *quiet* and real *quick*. The deal's supposed to go down at the end of the week. Already the Roarkes are getting twitchy. If it falls through—

Well, that's just *bad business*.

You don't think Bruno grabbed him? Maybe he's trying to squeeze you for a better deal.

He doesn't have the *horns* to try something like that.

Who'd you have watching him?

A *demi* by the name of *Benito*.

One of Tony's boys.

Lay off Tony. He didn't have anything to do with this.

I'd never figure you to let a *grudge* cloud clear thinking.

Come off it, Al. Any one of your own people could be selling you out. And you can't ask the Roarkes for help, because they'd suspect a *double-cross*. Or worse, see you as *weak*.

Right now, I'm the best friend you've got. You know I wasn't involved, because I was *tits up* when Lazlo disappeared.

Everyone else, you can trust about as much as you trust the *butt-end* of that stogie you're smoking.

That's what I like about you, Eddie. You're always thinking.

So I want you to *think* about *this*. You take care of this for me, and you and me are square.

You can go about your business... get yourself killed *again*... I won't dig you up.

All right...

...but we're quits after this.

Whatever you say, Eddie.

Three days.

Doesn't seem like such a long time.

Long enough for two demon families to put aside their differences and discuss business without tearing out each other's throats.

Big Al's making a play at solidifying his power, all nice and clean and *bloodless*.

Who am I kidding?

When it comes to demons, there's *always* blood.

Three days...

A long time to be dead.

GEHENNA ROOM
MEMBERS ONLY

Danny O'Brien's come a long way from his humble beginnings as a lowly thug in Aligheri's employ.

Few mortals climb the ladder, let alone strike out on their own to make it big.

But Danny—the bastard—did all right for himself.

This a private conversation, or can anybody join in?

Will you boys excuse me just a moment?

Don't go far, fellas. This *won't* take long.

Sorry to interrupt, Sophie. Didn't realize you were *entertaining*.

Don't mention it.

It's dangerous, you coming here.

You worried about me?

Not my job to worry about you any more, is it?

More like a hobby, really.

What do you want outta me, Eddie?

You drop off the face of the earth for days on end, then show up out of the blue all smiles and wisecracks.

What am I supposed to think?

Don't play stupid. You know I was lying in the mud with a new breathing hole cut in my neck.

What's more, you know it was your boyfriend who ordered the cutting.

Just what was I supposed to do? Danny wasn't going to carry your debt forever.

He might give somebody else a little rope, but not you.

Yeah. Not me.

I need you to set up a meeting between me and the Worm.

The Worm's not much for visitors these days.

He's been moving around a lot. Something's going on. Something that scares him.

He'll see me. It's important.

Isn't it always?

The only arrangements you need to make are for your funeral.

The next time I put you down, I'll make sure you stay there.

It's nice to have goals.

But last I heard, you pay off to Big Al, and right now I'm on the clock.

He won't look kindly on you clipping me before I get the job done.

For that matter, I wonder how Big Al would feel if he knew it was you who whacked me in the first place.

Tell him, why don't you? I may get kicked around by the demons every now and then, but I'm my own man these days.

Besides, Al understands these things. You think he couldn't find another *errand boy*?

He looks hard enough, he might even find someone who doesn't get in over his head betting on hayburners and bad poker hands.

Lucky for you, tonight I'm feeling charitable towards hard-luck cases.

But my patience has limits. I want the money you owe, or our next meeting won't be so civil.

In the meantime, I don't want you loitering around the club. My clientele gets uncomfortable around your type.

Three days.

I think he made me!

Told you to stop gawkin'.

What am I s'posed to do? Tony said to watch him, so's I'm watching.

You're about as subtle as bathtub hootch.

See what you made me do? I almost lost him!

Afternoon, Eddie.

Mind if I use the phone?

Help yourself.

click

Hello?

It's me.

Without info from the Worm, my best bet is tracking down the guy who was supposed to be babysitting Lazlo.

I'm lucky on two counts.

One—Benito's a creature of habit.

And two— he couldn't get laid without ponying up some cash.

Good to see you again, Eddie.

I'm here on business tonight.

Sweetheart, we're all here on business.

Benito here tonight?

Let's see... Don't recognize the name.

Funny. He's been coming here every Thursday for the last six years.

Second floor, on the right.

All right. Talk.

Talk about what? I got nothing to say.

The demon you were babysitting. What happened to him?

How should I know?

He got a breath of air that didn't stink of brimstone and decided to take a walk, take in a show.

You know I hate when you lie to me, Benny.

Reearrgh!!!

SSSSSSSS

Ahghh! Why'd you do that? Aggh!

That's nothing compared to what Tony's gonna do to you once he finds out you've been crossing Big Al.

What? No... No... Why would you tell him that?

Y'never know. I might be able to help you out. But you better give me something.

All right. All right. But you gotta help me, Eddie.

Things just got outta hand, y'know? I didn't realize they was gonna nab him.

Who?

I didn't recognize them. Figured them for out-of-towners.

I thought maybe he owed them money or something. I just wanted to make a little extra dough.

I didn't know he was some big-shot. They never tell me anything!

How was I supposed to know?

Big Al and Bruno, they buy and sell souls the way a greengrocer buys and sells cabbage.

Who am I to question if someone else wants to chisel in?

Souls?

Yeah. That's what this is about isn't it? That book Lazlo was carrying around.

You knew about that... right?

Get dressed.

W-Where are we going?

I dunno yet. I need to figure some things out. But I want to keep an eye on you.

Evening.

What are they doing here?

Wondered when you gents would show up.

Bruno's *curious*.

Yeah? Next time I see him, I'll tell him the one about the cat.

Seems to him, Big Al's acting a bit *peculiar*. We figured we'd check in with you to make sure everything's going all right with the business arrangement.

You don't think we're gonna sit idly by while Big Al pulls some kind of *grift*, do you?

Wish I could help you out, but I'm just here to pick up my pal.

If that's how it has to be.

Boys...

OOFH!

WHOOMP!

KRAK

Don't think I'm not *enjoying* this, but all I really want are some *answers*.

...

Hey, the boss never said nothin' about *drillin'* him.

BLAM!

BLAM!

BLAM!

Urgh...

urgh...

BLAM!

Ain't that always the way?

Lucky to be alive.

Better off dead.

CHAPTER

2

What do you mean, they're dead?!

Dead. They're dead. Just like I told ya. Dead.

Sheesh, boss. It ain't like I killed them. It was that guy you sent them after. He must have done it.

Sure. He whacked them.

What's his name again?

Eddie.

I want to see that sonuvabitch! I want him brought to me!

Boss—

And this time, send every man we've got to find him and bring—

Boss—

He's already here.

Funny thing about walking into a room full of angry demons.

It makes all your other worries just fade away.

Figure I'd save you gents the trouble of looking for me.

Bruno Roarke. Head of the second most powerful demon brood in the city.

Well, well, well...

He runs the low-brow rackets. Boxing. Betting. Bad booze.

He's in the middle of this negotiation with my boss, Alphonse Aligheri.

How ya been, Bruno?

Problem is, the big shot demon who was supposed to finalize the deal up and vanished.

Al wants me to find the broker before Bruno catches wind that something's wrong. A little late, if you ask me.

Of course, both Al and Bruno are expecting a double-cross.

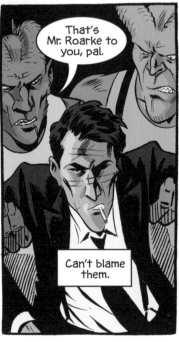

That's Mr. Roarke to you, pal.

Can't blame them.

They're demons, after all.

For a human, you got horns. I'll give you that. I send some of my boys—good boys—to have a polite conversation with you, and what do you do?

First of all, you know good and well there wasn't anything polite about my run-in with your boys.

And second of all—

I didn't do it.

So I'm supposed to believe they killed themselves?

Tommy went berserk—crazy or something. He killed the others and then plugged himself.

That's the dumbest thing I've ever heard. Tommy wouldn't have turned on my men. And he wouldn't have killed himself, neither.

Maybe you hadn't heard, but suicide's a sin.

Yeah? Maybe he got homesick.

Ya know, Eddie, there's no reason we can't be friends here.

Ya say you didn't whack my boys, I'll bite.

I'm a reasonable fella.

51

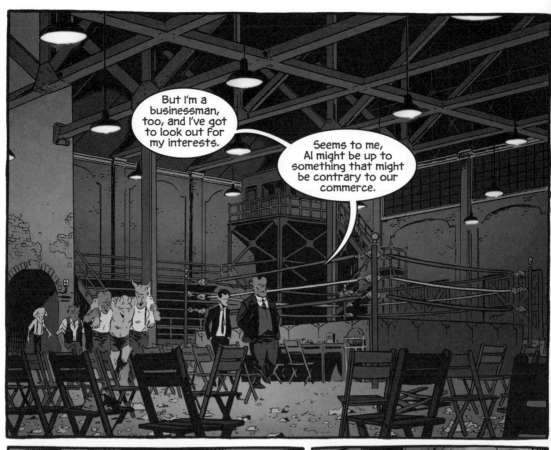

But I'm a businessman, too, and I've got to look out for my interests.

Seems to me, Al might be up to something that might be contrary to our commerce.

And you figure Al let me in on his scheme.

Precisely.

Wish I could help you.

Far as I know, whatever deal you and Big Al have brewing is going ahead as planned.

Call me a gentle soul, but I just didn't have the heart to tell him the negotiations were quickly going south, all on account of one stray big shot.

Eddie, Eddie, Eddie...

Ya oughta know better than to lie to me. I can smell mortal deception like a fart.

Maybe that stogie of yours is clogging your nostrils.

If you'd just spill Big Al's plan, we'd all be a whole lot happier, ya know.

Maybe, but if you just brought me out here to talk, then tell me—

What's with the goat?

G-goat?

An unpleasant necessity of business.

BEEE--!!

55

Funny thing about a summoned demon.

SKLORCH!!

It can only set foot on soil drenched in blood.

Bu... B-bu...

SKLOP!

But blood's never in short supply, really.

Fortunately, once you get a demon's blood boiling, it takes a bit for it to calm down.

He pretty much
killed me instantly.

Somebody *kill* him!

This way!

Get him!

Where'd he go?

I think he got away.

What're you talking about? He couldn't have gone far.

And did you see what he did to the big fella? Did ya?

I'll say it again. I think he got away.

Yeah. He must have given us the slip...

As far as curses go, I suppose I won the lottery.

Art...

Take a look at any one of my neighbors.

Things could be a lot worse than coming back from the dead over and over again.

Although lately I've been getting the feeling being dead might not be so bad after all.

Then again, it might be Hell.

Hi, Eddie.

Sophie.

You gonna stand there gawking or are you gonna invite me in for a drink?

I don't suppose Danny knows you're here.

I never took you for the naive type, Eddie.

The place hasn't changed much in the past few months.

Ugh! Where'd you get this stuff? It's awful.

It gets better with every sip.

Another?

Guess it's not as smooth as the fancy stuff you're used to now.

I didn't always have a view of the Avenue.

You've got a new scar.

More than one.

Any word from the Worm?

I told you. He doesn't want to see anyone right now. He's hiding from someone. Or something.

Then why are you even here?

Drop dead, Eddie!

A girl must be twisted to bed down with a cut-up freakshow like you.

What are you doing here, Tony?

I'm keeping an eye on you, of course. While you're knocking boots, I'm looking out for Big Al's interests.

Didn't know Al had interests in watching me sleep.

Maybe he should take up a hobby.

Get dressed, lover boy.

So, where are we going, Tony?

To see Benito.

Already seen him.

Yeah. I know. Last night.

What happened, Eddie? The Worm cut you loose and now you actually gotta do your own footwork?

Something like that.

Worm probably doesn't like the way you've been putting it to his sister.

Does this little trip have a point or are you just trying to live vicariously through me?

What happened with Benito last night? What did he tell you?

He wasn't much help. Why?

Well, somebody thought he knew something.

So the question is, when you talked to him, was he cooperative?

Or did you have to convince him?

Come off it, Tony. You know I didn't do this. I might have roughed him up a little, but—

Let me guess.

Nothing like this.

What's this all about? If you think I killed your Flunkie, you're wrong.

If you brought me here to kill me, get on with it.

I've got places to be.

If I were you, I'd start paying a little more attention to the job, and a little less attention to Danny O'Brien's girl.

You aren't careful, you're gonna end up in an alley where no one will be able to find your body.

I'm touched you care so much.

Only thing I care about is making sure the boss doesn't get screwed over by the likes of you.

come on, Eddie.

come on, Eddie...

CHAPTER

3

Looks like a *full house* to me!

Aww, *applesauce!*

That's four hands in a row, Rags. You wouldn't be grifting us, wouldya?

Come on, Fellas. Dontcha think we gots enough to worry about?

What with the whole *cease-fire* with the Roarkes ready to fall apart any minute, you'd think you boys wouldn't be so quick to accuse your old buddy, Rags.

Maybe so, but maybe this truce has got ya bored without any skulls to bust.

Maybe all that free time got ya thinking about earning a little extra bread.

Look, I ain't above cheating any more than you are, but tonight, I'm relying on pure—

Hkkg!

Heard you were looking for me.

You're a hard man to find.

When I want to be.

I didn't know better, I'd say you were hiding from *someone* or *something*.

What's wrong, you think curiosity's gonna pick this week to finally kill the cat?

You're the one to talk, the way you're sticking your nose where it don't belong.

You know good and well this deal between Big Al and Bruno Roarke is souring faster than goat's milk on a hot day.

Once the fighting starts again... well, it just ain't safe.

That's why you've been laying low? You want to sit this one out?

Funny. I didn't think it was ever safe for guys like us.

I thought you and Big Al were quits.

It's *temporary.*

Sure, sure.

Sounds like you know why I'm here already.

Why don't you tell me what I need to know so you can get back to your *hiding*.

That any way to treat me when I'm risking my neck just to help you out?

Come off it. The only reason you're helping me is because *Sophie* asked you.

What? We're not pals anymore?

All right. All right.

So somebody pinched the high order demon who's here to help the *Aligheris* and *Roarkes* play nice. And you need to find him.

Ever get the feeling Big Al's not telling you everything?

Don't be a *wise guy*. Spill it, would ya?

I'll tell you...

...but you ain't gonna like it.

Crowley's Creek.

Never a nice neighborhood, not even on the best of days. Now it's downright eerie.

Few years back, it was overrun with demons.

The *Verlochin*.

They're the family that makes the other demons afraid of the boogeyman.

I don't even like thinking about what went on in the cellars in these parts when the Verlochin were in charge.

Of course, the Aligheris and the Roarkes sent them packing, back when Big Al and Bruno had a common enemy to keep them occupied.

They're long gone now.

Good riddance.

Unless they're back.

SKREEEEE

BLAM!

Aw...

You're an odd one.

You're always coming and going.

You never stay.

Not for long.

What is this place?

Once it was *everything*. Now it is *nothing*.

But you know that. It's why you're here, isn't it?

I don't know what—

I don't know.

But they were ready for me.

Waiting for me.

Somebody warned them I was coming.

Mortals, though.

Not the Verlochin's style.

Small favors and all.

So if the book-keeper was here, they sure moved him before my daring rescue.

Another *dead end.*

So much for *Lazlo*.

Tell me this isn't what I think it is...

What?

Got nothing to say?

I figured you'd make an exception for me.

 Eddie! You thought right, kid. Been wondering when you'd turn up.

You should really try this acupuncture business. Does wonders for your aching muscles.

 No, thanks.

Always work with you, eh, Eddie? So, what did you find? Where's Lazlo?

He's *dead*.

 Ow! Hey! Careful back there!

You say dead? That ain't good.

 No good at all. Could set things back quite a bit. And the Roarkes are sick of waiting.

Bruno's gonna want blood for sure.

 Find *anything* else?

 Didn't know I was looking for anything else.

Ratta--ta--ratta---tat

What the—

Guess Bruno's more impatient than you thought!

KSH!

And here I was hoping to keep from dying for the rest of the day.

CHAPTER

4

I don't
believe it.

For once
I didn't die.

Never thought I'd be so
glad to find myself hiding
behind a big, naked demon.

Y'okay,
boss?

Get me
my clothes,
wouldya?

And
another
stoagie.

Guess Bruno's
figured out your
negotiations are
bust-o.

Or maybe he
just got tired
of waiting.

Any sign of them?

They're long gone.

Let them run, for all the good it'll do.

I want this stitched up, Tony. Real quick.

Like a bunny.

So that's how it plays out?

After all your bragging about a peaceful future, you're gonna jump up and down on Bruno 'til he squeals.

It's Bruno what started this, not me. I went to a lot of trouble to arrange this deal.

Least that old blowhard coulda done was weather a few bumps along the way.

For all I know, Bruno nabbed Lazlo himself.

Bruno's not stupid enough to go against you without a reason—

—and he's not smart enough to pull something like that off right under your nose.

If he wants to hit the mattresses, it's because he thinks *you* double-crossed him.

Just what kind of deal was this, anyway?

Whatever it is, it must be pretty important for the Roarkes to try to take you out.

Doesn't matter now, I suppose.

Been a long time since the city's seen a war.

These things have a way of spilling over into the real world. A lot of mortals are gonna get caught in the crossfire.

A lot of *innocents*.

No such thing, Eddie, and you know it.

If you could have finished Bruno off so easy, why bother with a peace offering in the first place?

The two of you get in a pissing contest, it won't matter how big and bad you are, it's gonna cost you.

98

99

"...no such thing as innocence."

What do you want, Eddie?

I need a word with you.

I'll give you *two*.

Get.

Lost.

Eddie... Danny's—

I'm not worried about Danny.

I get the feeling he'll have his hands full doing Al's dirty work soon enough.

Funny...

...I thought you were taking care of Al's dirty laundry. Guess you did a good job, too. Your obligation to me has been squared.

But I seem to remember something about me asking you not to show your *ugly mug* around here again.

Hahaha hahaha!

Ratta-tat ratta

Ratta-tat-ratta

Yeah, the city can be a real unfriendly place in the middle of a gang war.

CAW!

Within three yards of the front door, my blood runs cold, and a knot of ice swells in my breadbasket.

I can *feel* them.

And apparently they can sense me.

Never let it be said the Verlochin underestimate the value of cheap theatrics.

I can hear voices coming from somewhere within. I focus on the sound. Follow it.

One wrong turn in... this place and I might be lost forever.

But there has to be some other way. *Please!* Can't I make this up to you somehow?

Come now, Oliver. Begging's so unseemly.

And, I'm afraid, quite pointless.

Come in, Eddie. We're almost done.

Just like Big Al and Bruno, the Verlochin trade in souls.

But they're the only family still using *curses* to punish those who step out of line.

Everything changes at one point or another.

I'm telling you. Things have changed.

But we've honored our bargain, and we expected you to do the same.

Believe me, I should know.

But I didn't expect anything like this. How could I?

Ignorance is a weakness, not an excuse.

But my wife... She's going to have a baby.

We were going to have a *family*.

You're *still* going to have a family.

But... but...

Where did you get this?

Does it matter?

The page spooked them, which made me all the more uncomfortable.

It's a listing of damned souls, right?

People who sold their souls. To Al. To Bruno.

To you.

So why would someone be willing to kill for a book of lost souls?

Your assumptions are amusing, Eddie. The book is so much more than that.

See? Mortal souls listed alongside the name of the demon who brokered the deal.

The **true** name.

That supposed to mean something to me?

Because I'm drawing a blank.

Speaking a demon's true name has great power. Power to force a demon to do one's bidding.

All right, so the book's worth something.

Maybe this isn't about spoiling Big Al's truce after all.

You don't seem overly worried. Your names are listed, too, aren't they?

Hardly a concern.

The book is written in a language only a pure demon can decipher. Without translation, control would be random at best.

And what's to stop another demon from using the true name against you?

Hitting a nerve with one of these guys is next to impossible.

But when you do, it's almost worth the price of admission.

Almost.

Still, makes sense.

Someone steals the book and kidnaps the bookkeeper to try to force him to translate. Only, the demon's too stubborn to cooperate.

And if they needed a demon to translate...

...that would mean the book and Lazlo were most likely snagged by someone mortal.

Someone human.

Been nice visiting with you. We'll have to do this again real soon.

Something else on your mind, Eddie?

Soul-trading used to be neat and clean and easy.

Prick your finger, sign the dotted line, follow the rules, and pay up when your time comes.

But like I said, the Verlochin use curses to enforce their will.

The place I go... when I die...

So, you remember.

We were starting to believe you were too dense to ever open your eyes.

Either that or you're much less curious than we gave you credit for.

It's not Hell, not exactly, and it can't be—

No, it can't.

Then... where? I've seen someo—

Something.

So many people think the *Fall* from Heaven was like falling out of bed.

A shooting star, perhaps... or poor Icarus with his melted wings...

But it was slow. *Painful.*

An *agony* lasting eons.

115

When our purchase on the heavenly realms began to slip through our fingers, we sought a new refuge.

And for a time, we settled in a land beneath the notice of the Host.

But we were not alone. We found the ruins of a kingdom within the mist, and it served as a bitter reminder.

Like us, it had once been great, but had gone to waste.

And *others* already dwelled there, at least temporarily.

The restless dead—those who had lost their way from the earthly world to the Majestic Gates.

We were becoming shadows of our former selves.

So in the shadows we bred and we grew strong again.

Until the shadows would no longer hold us.

We made ourselves known to our neighbors. Offered them friendship and guidance and hope.

And we lied.

For if we could not have Heaven, why should they?

Once again, we felt strong and proud, and we instructed our students to rebuild the kingdom in our image.

We knew we could not hide forever, though, and when the Host came for us, they would destroy us forever for corrupting those who were lost.

So we found even deeper places, and there we built ourselves a new home.

When the Host finally arrived, they found only our leavings. And they worked their wardings to bar us from that realm forever.

So you hid, like roaches scurrying away from the light.

We found a place where even the Host dared not tread.

And the... others... the people...

Lost souls.

You sons of bitches! You knew! This whole time, you knew!

You know that won't work here, Eddie, not in this place. If you're trying to prove a point, you're wasting—

Have a seat, Eddie. We still have a lot to discuss.

Lemme through, will ya? I got news.

Hey, outta the way. We got *trouble*. The Roarkes just took down one of Danny's clubs.

Far as they're concerned, Danny's in the same boat as Big Al.

You'll get your chance, pip-squeak. Right now the boss has a visitor.

Let's see if I'm clear on this.

All of a sudden, you're getting cold feet.

Or *whatever* it is that gets cold on a guy like you.

See, that just doesn't work for me.

You came to me because you knew we could help each other. Now that things are getting a little rough on the streets, you wanna cut your losses.

But the way I see it, you're in it for the long haul, just like me.

If Big Al or Tony finds out...

Heck, even if Eddie finds out...

Don't you worry about them.

CHAPTER

5

...s'wut I tole 'im, I did... tole 'im wut 'e could do wif 'is fancy...

Eh?

'Ey, buddy.

You don' wanna go in there.

There's *monsters* in there.

That right?

Guess I got the right place then.

Monsters...

Yeah...

I got the right place, all right.

This is the best hiding place you could find? I thought you knew *every* nook and cranny of the city.

You got a guy out front who's pretty much telling anyone who passes by this place is full of *monsters*.

Lucky for me, not too many people are just *passing by* in this neighborhood.

Not unless they're looking for *trouble*.

125

That what this is about *Eddie?* You looking for trouble?

Guess that depends on the answers I get.

You outta your mind, showing up here like this? We're in the middle of a *war*, for chrissakes. What if someone followed you?

You know how *valuable* a guy like me could be to the Aligheris? To the Roarkes?

Feeling *important*, are you?

You're not the only one with *resources.*

How'd you find me anyway?

Guess we should cut to the chase, yeah?

Why'd you set me up?

W—what do you mean?

Crowley's Creek. They *knew* I was coming. They were ready for me.

I didn't have anything to do with that.

You sure about that?

Of course, I'm sure. I wouldn't... eh?

What's that?

126

Salt.

What are ya gonna do with—Yaaaaargghh!

It burns!

Figured it would.

SSSSSSSSSS

SSSSSSSSSSSS

Sure you don't want to rethink your story?

You sonuvabitch! All I have to do is think about it, and you're as good as eaten alive!

I think I'll be just fine, leastways until I hear you out.

All right! All right! But ya gotta believe me, Eddie, I never wanted you to get hurt.

I found out about the deal—about the book—and I figured I could make myself a deal.

My name's in the book, Eddie. I figured I could force the verlochin to let me out of the contract... to break the curse.

But you didn't think you could do it on your own... and you figured you could make a little scratch for yourself in the process.

Who'd you sell the information to?

You already know.

Yeah, I guess I do. I didn't come here for information. Not this time.

More than anything, I came to tell you, you cross me again, and that curse of yours is gonna be the least of your worries.

127

No guards.

Maybe he ain't here.

Naw, he's just too overconfident for his own good.

He's here.

And he's all alone.

This is how *demons* make war.

You must be crazy, Tony. You know that?

Never knew why Al would want a *mortal* watching his back.

Maybe he'd rather bank on somebody what's crazy instead of stupid.

Wha—

KSH

CRK

SNAP

CRK

133

Forbidden by who? The *Devil*?

Don't worry about the Devil. Worry about *me*.

Let me know as soon as he starts squawking. He looks pretty tough, so it may take a while.

I'll be upstairs.

You should be *proud* of yourself. You're about to become the most important demon in history.

I gotta hand it to you, Danny...

You've got *ambition*.

Maybe not a lot in the way of smarts, but ambition you got in spades.

Eddie.

Wish I could say I'm glad to see you.

The pleasure's all mine, Danny. Put the book on the table.

Looking for this?

I always figured a .22 for a *twist's* gun, but y'know, it kinda suits you.

Sit down.

I want you to think for just a second, Eddie. Think about what you're doing... and what you're passing up.

Your name's in here, too.

That's right. Now you see where I'm going with this, don't ya.

All we need is for a demon to crack the code, and you can get your *life* back. You can get *anything* you ever wanted.

Tempting. And what do you get out of this?

What do you think? I get to crawl out from under Big Al's thumb for a change. The demons will listen to me for awhile instead of the other way around.

And you think some demon's just gonna hand you the keys to the castle, is that it?

We'll just see.

Anything I want, huh?

You ever consider that might not be such a good thing for *you*?

I'll take my *chances*.

And here I thought I was the one who placed bad bets.

Why don't you hand me that book and we'll get this over with.

So that's it, huh? You're just going to take the book and *kill* me?

What? You still sore about that little incident in the alley?

Sophie's name's in the book, too.

See, Eddie, the Worm told me all about this book. All he asked in return was that I help him rid himself of his curse.

And that I help his *sister* reclaim her soul.

In a way, you should thank me. I'm helping the woman you *love* better herself. Doesn't that just warm your heart?

And once she gets her soul back, you think she could possibly *love* a scumbag like you?

You shouldn't have come here. Not alone.

BLAM BLAM BLAM

Who said anything about being alone?

What's that supposed to mean?

Danny!

Cunning. Cruel. Devious.

You would have made a good *demon*, Mr. O'Brien.

Touché, Eddie.

I didn't have any beef with your family. Only with the *Aligheris* and *Roarkes*. You could *benefit* from this. We could make some kind of *deal*.

We set the terms of any bargain in which we're involved, Mr. O'Brien. And we would *never* let this book be used by a mortal, not even against our enemies.

But perhaps there is an *arrangement* you might find agreeable.

Eddie's still *valuable* to us, after all.

The choice is yours, Mr. O'Brien. You can come with us, or...

Ain't it always the way?

Nothing brings a family together like a *funeral*.

Ashes to ashes and all that.

In a way, I almost feel sorry for *Lazlo*. He was just doing his job when he got caught up in this plot to overthrow the *families*.

Of course, he was a *demon* himself, so my sympathies only run so deep.

As we send our brother, *Lazlo*, back to the *infernal realm*, I would like to offer each of you the opportunity to wish him well and honor him.

Who will be the first to spill blood in our brother's name?

No thanks. I've had enough of goats for a while.

Hey, Eddie! Wait up!

Your boss looks *preoccupied* right now, Tony.

Tell him to stop by *my place* sometime and I'll give him the *book*.

Yeah. Nothing brings a family together...

...like *death.*

Back again. Back again. Over and over, you come back.

Have they sent you back for me this time?

I'll not give them to you, not without a *fight.*

Time passes... differently here.

Eh?

Yes. Different for everyone. Moments for some.

Eternity for others.

I'm not here for you.

Take me to *her.*

Suit yourself. I guess you'll be taking the *book* and leaving.

If you don't mind.

You did a good thing for me, Eddie.

You didn't have to find the book and put an end to the war, but you did. That's why I wanted you to have the club. You deserve it.

Looks like some of the pages are *missing.*

That right? I wonder what could have *happened* to them. I hope they don't fall into the *wrong hands* or anything.

I'm sure you gents can show yourselves out. Oh, and one more thing. This club...

...it's got a *no demons* allowed policy now. Get me?

Ma...

147

#1 ISSUE
DEBUTS
MAY 2017

FOR
ONLY $1

As you might imagine, Eddie's troubles are far from over, and they ain't all brought about by demons. Running the Gehenna Room is headache aplenty, but when a pal from the bad old days shows up seeking a favor, the needle really starts to twist. Eddie's friend has a secret, and with Eddie's help, he plans on beating the demons at their own game.

TO BE CONTINUED MAY 2017
IN THE ONGOING SERIES

DAMNED™

"*The Damned* is a richly rendered, gangster tale with an extra demonic twist. Fiendish entertainment at its best!"
– Amy Chu
(*Poison Ivy, Girls Night Out*)

"Bunn, Hurtt and Crabtree must have made some kind of demon-pact in order to create a book that is as entertaining, engaging and gorgeous as *The Damned*."
– Declan Shalvey
(*Injection, All-Star Batman, Moon Knight*)

"Bunn, Hurtt, & Crabtree at their most hardcore... you can feel the heat of the hellfire and gunpowder."
– Sam Humphries
(*Green Lanterns, Jonesy*)

"Dark, dirty, demon noir at its best."
–Matt Kindt
(*Dept. H, Mind MGMT*)

CULLEN BUNN is the writer of comic books such *The Sixth Gun*, *Helheim*, and *The Tooth* for Oni Press. He has also written titles including *Harrow County* (Dark Horse), *Uncanny X-Men*, and *Deadpool and The Mercs For Money* (Marvel).

Cullen claims to have worked as an Alien Autopsy Specialist, Rodeo Clown, Pro Wrestling Manager, and Sasquatch Wrangler. He has fought for his life against mountain lions and performed on stage as the World's Youngest Hypnotist. Buy him a drink sometime, and he'll tell you all about it.

His website is cullenbunn.com. · Twitter: @cullenbunn

BRIAN HURTT is an artist/writer who has spent most of his career working on collaborative creator-owned projects.

His first such collaboration was in 2006 when Brian teamed with writer Cullen Bunn to create the Prohibition-era, monster-noir, cult classic, *The Damned*.

A few years later the two teamed up again to create *The Sixth Gun*—a weird-west, epic supernatural fantasy. This fan-favorite series ran 50 issues and included two spin-off mini-series that Brian co-wrote with Cullen Bunn as well as the spin-off mini-series, *Valley of Death*, in which he was the sole writer.

Brian also contributes to the popular webcomic *Table Titans*. He is the writer and artist of the *Table Titans* stories "Whispers of Dragons" and "Road to Embers".

Brian lives and works in St. Louis, Missouri.

His website is Brihurtt.com · Twitter: @brihurtt
Instagram: @brihurtt · tabletitans.com

BILL CRABTREE'S career as a colorist began in 2003 with the launch of Image Comic's *Invincible* and *Firebreather*. He was nominated for a Harvey Award for his work on *Invincible*, and he went on to color the first 50 issues of what would become a flagship Image Comics title. He continues to color *Firebreather*, which was recently made into a feature film on Cartoon Network, *Godland*, and *Jack Staff*.

Perhaps the highlight of his comics career, his role as colorist on the Oni Press series *The Sixth Gun* began with issue 6, and has since been described as "like Christmas morning, but with guns."